FOR

DUMMIES®

POCKET EDITION

by Yvonne Jeffery, Liz Barclay,
and Michael Grosvenor

WILEY

Wiley Publishing, Inc.

Green Living For Dummies, Pocket Edition

Published by
Wiley Publishing, Inc.
111 River St.
Hoboken, NJ 07030-5774
www.wiley.com

Table of Contents

Introduction

● ●

*I*f you're interested in the environment, want to know a little more about why so many people are concerned about the future of the planet, or want to know what you can do to help, *Green Living For Dummies* is the book for you.

We don't pretend to know how to save the planet. Even if you put the world's leading environmental scientists, researchers, and politicians together in one room, you'd have a great deal of trouble getting them to agree on exactly what to do first and how to do it. However, almost everyone agrees on one thing: that we need to start taking action now in order to stop using the Earth's resources faster than the planet can replenish them.

Many people argue for the need to take seriously drastic action, and they're partly right. Industries need to stop polluting, governments need to support clean alternative energy, and communities at every level need to get onboard with waste reduction. But that doesn't mean that people should ignore the very real gains that every single individual can make toward the goal of a cleaner, greener world.

Just as you can't expect industries, governments, and communities to change overnight, you shouldn't expect to make instant changes yourself. But small steps, consistently taken, *will* make a difference. This book shows you how.

Icons Used in This Book

A quick flip through this book will reveal some small pictures in the margins. Here's a primer on the meaning of each icon:

This icon is a target to aim for! It offers special information that could provide some handy assistance.

You may have read it already or heard it before, but the information highlighted by this icon is worth keeping in mind for future use.

This icon highlights actions that you can take now or plan to do in the future to make you an especially greener person.

With this icon, you find information that explains how things have happened — or how they could happen in the future.

Where to Go from Here

You've got your minibook copy of *Green Living For Dummies*. Now what? This minibook is a reference, so if you need information on green cleaning supplies, head to Chapter 2. Or if you're interested in finding out about eating a healthy, green diet, go straight to Chapter 4. Or heck, start with Chapter 1 and read the chapters in order . . . you rebel. If you want even more advice on green living, from finding the most ethically produced clothing to raising green kids, check out the full-size version of *Green Living For Dummies* — simply head to your local book seller or go to www.dummies.com!

Chapter 1
Being Greener for the Good of People and the Planet

● ●

In This Chapter

▶ Exploring choices and the benefits of change

▶ Making small changes every day for big, green gains

● ●

*W*hat, exactly, does *green* or *sustainable living* mean? Different people use different definitions, but it all comes down to one fundamental concept: The Earth's resources shouldn't be depleted faster than they can be replenished. From that concept comes everything else, including caring for the environment, animals and other living things, your health, your local community, and communities around the world.

Understanding the Impact of Your Choices

Right now, the planet's resources are being depleted far faster than they can be replenished. Fossil fuels such as oil are becoming more difficult and more expensive to bring out of the ground, and their reserves are dwindling. Burning fossil fuels to provide energy for homes, vehicles, and industries emits carbon dioxide and other greenhouse gases along with pollutants that affect the health of the planet and its people.

Other resources are in trouble too, including water. In some parts of the United States, drought conditions are becoming more common and more widespread. Decreasing the demand that people place on water sources is essential in order to continue having enough water to go around.

Thankfully, it's not too late to make the changes that the planet and its people need for a safe, healthy, prosperous, and compassionate future.

A useful way to understand your impact on the environment is to measure your *ecological footprint,* which is the land needed to support your consumption of goods and resources. Think of it as a way of describing the amount of land required to farm your food, mine your energy sources, transport your goods and services, and hold your waste. You make decisions every day that have an impact on the planet: choosing between the car and local rapid transit, for example, or selecting local or organic fresh food instead of packaged, processed food that has been transported long distances. Think about the impact that each individual decision has, and weigh the pros and cons of your everyday actions.

You can measure your own ecological footprint simply by visiting the Earth Day Network Web site at www.earthday.net and entering some information about your lifestyle (such as the size and type of your home, how often you eat meat and processed foods, and how many miles you drive each week).

Recognizing the Rewards of a Sustainable Lifestyle

As you begin to make your life greener, you'll see benefits well beyond the immediate green ones. You'll discover that being green can improve your life in all kinds of areas. Here are just a few of the major benefits of a sustainable lifestyle:

- ✔ **Saving money:** Consuming less of any commodity — from electricity to water to clothes — means that you pay less, too. You'll have lower utility bills and a budget with breathing room when you take actions such as buying quality items that last a long time and even growing some of your own food.

- ✔ **Encouraging profits:** When you support green and ethical businesses such as stores and financial institutions, you help them to stay profitable enough to continue acting in environmentally and socially responsible ways. You also send a message to less responsible companies that they need to clean up their acts.

- ✔ **Boosting health:** If you walk and cycle instead of driving and if you reduce the amount of chemicals in your food, home, and garden, you can improve your cardiovascular health, boost your immune system, build stronger muscles, and have cleaner lungs.

- ✔ **Leaving a legacy:** The opportunity to protect what's vital about the planet for future generations is perhaps the most important benefit of all. If you consume only what you need, reduce your trash, live more naturally, and invest carefully, you do a great deal to leave a planet that will benefit people and wildlife for centuries to come.

Changing What You Can as You Can

Although you can't change the world and save the planet single-handedly overnight, you can make a difference — and you can start right away with whatever budget and time you have available.

The best strategy is to take change one step at a time and implement small changes when and as you can. Also, assess where you're starting from (calculating your ecological footprint is one way to measure this; see "Understanding the Impact of Your Choices," earlier in this chapter) and figure out what you can do to counter your effect through carbon offsetting if you can't yet make the changes you want to make.

Adopting the four primary green strategies

Here are four green living strategies that you can implement in a variety of ways to contribute to the solutions that the planet needs:

- **Reduce consumption.** Anything that you do to decrease the amount of the Earth's resources that you use — from choosing goods with less packaging to turning down your home's thermostat a few degrees in the winter — helps you to lead a more sustainable life.

✔ **Choose carefully.** Thinking about a product's entire life cycle — from manufacture to disposal — helps you make the greenest choices possible. You protect not only the environment but also the people involved in the manufacturing process.

✔ **Opt for renewable resources.** Replacing your use of nonrenewable resources (such as energy based on fossil fuels) with renewable resources (such as solar or wind energy) is a very powerful green action — and it may be easier than you think.

✔ **Repair when needed.** There are plenty of ways that you can help to fix the damage that's already been done to the environment, from supporting tree-planting projects to helping out with community programs at home and around the world.

Taking those first small steps

Making small changes as and when you can puts you firmly on the road to living a much greener lifestyle. Decide what your priorities are: Think about where it would be easiest for you to begin. Start there, and work up to the bigger or more difficult issues.

You can start by replacing your light bulbs as they burn out with compact fluorescent models and replacing your cleaning supplies as they run out with environmentally friendly ones.

 Another strategy that's super-easy to implement is to buy items with less packaging. Consider, for example, what would happen if you bought toilet paper in double rolls, which contain twice as much toilet paper in a roll as regular-size rolls do. That cuts in half the number of cardboard tubes inside the rolls, and it also decreases the amount of plastic that's used to wrap the packages! If you recycle the cardboard tubes that remain, even better. And if you slit the plastic wrap open only at the top of the package, you can reuse the wrap, maybe as a trash bag.

Making Your Greenbacks Even Greener

When it comes to spending and saving money, your dollars can go a long way toward greening your lifestyle. Start with the necessities of life — choosing what you eat and what you wear — and assess how you can do both in ways that are both socially and environmentally responsible. Then expand these issues to the banking arena, looking at where you can park your money and how you can invest your savings to help you as well as your community and the planet.

Shopping greenly and ethically

Shopping is a great opportunity to make your lifestyle more sustainable. Choose the greenest options available to you, such as food produced using as few chemicals as possible, grown locally in season, and transported over as short a distance as possible to reduce the amount of fuel used. Other green options include clothes made from organically produced materials, goods made from recycled materials rather than resources that have to be mined from the earth, secondhand or vintage goods, and those made from biodegradable materials.

Ask stores whether the workers, producers, suppliers, and farmers involved in the production chain are paid fairly, have good working conditions, and can sustain their production (meaning that they have enough left after feeding themselves and their families to maintain their premises or buy new equipment and seeds). Avoiding goods produced using child labor or in sweatshop working conditions also may be a priority for you.

Animal welfare is a growing concern as well; consider choosing meat and dairy products that come from animals raised in humane conditions rather than intensively farmed, overcrowded pens and cages.

Support your local community socially and economically by buying your food, gifts, crafts, home items, and clothes from local producers and businesses. If that's not possible, look for Fairtrade-certified products that assure you that growers and producers were treated fairly.

Saving, investing, and donating wisely

When it comes to saving or investing your money, you can make it work for both you and the environment by choosing where you bank. An increasing number of financial institutions offer savings accounts or investment services that support green, sustainable, and socially responsible programs, often in your own community. Some financial institutions not only offer these accounts but conduct their day-to-day operations in a socially and environmentally responsible way.

The kinds of financial programs that these institutions offer may include using the money in savings and investment accounts to leverage low-interest loans to help local businesses improve their energy efficiency or to build alternative energy infrastructure such as solar or wind power. Programs also may help nonprofit organizations set up work or self-employment training programs or affordable housing initiatives.

When it comes to long-term investments such as mutual funds or the stock market, you can go green there, too, by opting for an ethical or green fund that invests in companies that meet various environmental or social criteria or by investing directly in the companies themselves. Some green-minded investment accounts ask you to accept a lower interest rate on your savings in exchange for these positive effects, but for others, you have the opportunity for just as much of a return as you would get if your money were in conventional accounts.

Venturing Out into the World

The greenest thing you can possibly do when it comes to traveling and transportation is simply not to go — vacation locally instead of halfway around the world, for example, or work from home instead of commuting. That's not always possible, practical, or even desirable, however, so this section looks at ways to get on the road while minimizing your impact on the environment.

Getting around

Transportation, particularly passenger vehicles and planes, emit a tremendous amount of carbon and other pollutants into the atmosphere, where they contribute to climate change and a range of health problems.

As a consumer, you can make a difference by reducing the amount that you fly or drive. Vacation locally, for example, or work from home one day a week if possible. When you have to travel, choose more-sustainable methods of transportation, including local bus, rapid transit, and train services. These methods of transportation still emit pollutants, but because they carry more people at one time, their emissions per person are much lower than if the passengers were all in their own cars.

Traveling mindfully

Before you book your next vacation, consider where you want to go in the world and why, and think about whether you can achieve the same effect closer to home (to cut down on your greenhouse gas emissions) or in a more ecologically friendly way (like by taking the train instead of flying).

Traveling widely can broaden your horizons and facilitate better understanding between cultures. So consider taking fewer long-distance vacations and making them last longer in order to get the best possible investment from the greenhouse gas emissions that your travel is responsible for.

To take your vacation deeper into environmental or social responsibility, consider an eco-tourism trip that provides insight into the local ecosystem or a volunteer vacation in which you spend part or much of your time on a project that helps either the local people or the environment.

You can help to compensate for the greenhouse gas emissions that your travel produces through *carbon offsetting,* paying for or participating in programs that reduce the carbon in the atmosphere. Many of those programs involve planting trees; others fund research into alternative or cleaner conventional technologies.

Chapter 2
Making Your Home Healthy and Efficient

. . . .

In This Chapter

▶ Focusing on home heating and cooling

▶ Using and maintaining appliances for top efficiency

▶ Conserving water

▶ Ditching chemical products

. . . .

Developing green habits around your home can reduce your impact on the environment in a major way — and they come with some great side benefits, including improved health and lower utility bills.

This chapter provides tips and tricks for eco-friendly living in your home. From your home's biggest energy draws (heating and cooling) to more moderate ones (various home appliances), we tell you what to pay attention to and how to reduce your impact on the environment. We also cover natural alternatives to chemical-filled household products and items that you're likely to use daily. Add a little water conservation (or a lot!) and some simple changes that you can make around the house, and this chapter is chock-full of useful information for greening up your home.

Managing Your Home's Temperature

Many living areas in homes are hotter than they need to be in winter and cooler than they need to be in summer. This section shares some easy ways to manage the temperature inside your home in a better, smarter way.

Whether it's spring, summer, fall, or winter, some energy-saving tips work all year long. Try the following actions to save energy year-round:

- ✔ **Add weather-stripping to doors and windows.**

- ✔ **Tuck insulating foam inserts behind switch plates and face plates of electrical outlets on exterior walls.** These products are readily available at home-improvement centers.

- ✔ **Install awnings that shade windows in summer but retract in winter to let you take advantage of the sun's warmth.**

- ✔ **Plant deciduous trees (that lose their leaves in winter) to shade the house in summer and let sunlight through in winter.**

- ✔ **Control the amount of heating or cooling going into rooms in your home that you're not using by fully or partially closing the forced-air registers, for example.** Don't completely block off the heating in particular, because you don't want anything to freeze.

- ✔ **Use kitchen and bathroom ventilating fans as little as possible to avoid sending too much heated or cooled air out of the house.**

In the summer, set your thermostat to about 78°F when you're in the house during the day, and turn the air-conditioning off completely when you're away from the house for an extended period. In the winter, set your thermostat to no more than about 70°F to 72°F when you're in the house during the day, and set it to 65°F at night and when you're away from the house. A programmable thermostat is the easiest way to manage these temperatures automatically.

Making Appliances More Efficient and Eco-Friendly

From the kitchen to the laundry room to the basement or utility room, you have appliances throughout your home. Keeping them clean and well-maintained helps them to function more efficiently for longer periods of time.

Water heater

There's not a lot that you can do in terms of cleaning the interior of your water heater, but you can take measures to limit how hard it has to work. Energy-saving measures for water heaters include the following:

- ✔ **Check that the setting on your water heater isn't overheating your water.** A setting of 120°F suits most uses, but double-check the owner's manual for your dishwasher, which may require a higher setting. Don't set your water-heater thermostat below 115°F; in some cases, this can lead to the growth of mold within the water heater.

- ✔ **Wrap the first 6 feet of pipe leading out of your water heater with insulating foam.**

✔ **Wrap the water heater in a foil blanket for insulation.** Follow the instructions very carefully when you install it to avoid blocking vents or controls. Check your heater's instructions to ensure that adding insulation is permitted for your model.

Clothes washer and dryer

Follow these recommendations for making what's perhaps one of your most tedious chores more enjoyable because it's earth-friendly:

✔ **Wash your laundry in cold water.** Stick to hot water for items such as sheets and towels, particularly if someone in the family has been ill. Only hot water kills hangers-on such as germs and dust mites. Even with a hot or warm wash, choose a cold rinse.

✔ **Do the laundry only when you have a full load.** Even with a full load, don't overload the washing machine.

✔ **Line-dry your clothes.**

✔ **If you need to use the dryer, dry full (not partial) loads only, and dry your clothes for the minimum time possible.**

✔ **If you have to iron, do it when clothes are still slightly damp or use a spray bottle to dampen them rather than a steam iron.** A steam iron uses energy heating up the water in its tank.

Dishwasher

According to the U.S. Department of Energy, an Energy Star–rated dishwasher (www.energystar.gov) saves nearly 5,000 gallons of water a year compared to washing dishes by hand and uses less than half as much energy, which can cut utility bills by more than $40 a year.

If you go with the dishwasher over hand-washing, consider these recommendations to reduce your environmental impact:

- ✔ Skip the pre-rinse if your dishwasher gets the dishes clean without it.

- ✔ Consult your owner's manual for the way to place items in the dishwasher for the most-efficient cleaning.

- ✔ Only run the dishwasher when it's full.

- ✔ Use the dishwasher's no-heat air-drying option if it has one. If it doesn't, turn the dishwasher off as soon as it has finished washing, before it starts the drying cycle.

- ✔ Clean out the drain filter monthly both to keep the dishwasher clean and to maintain its efficiency.

Conserving Water Manually

Water is one of the Earth's most precious resources — it literally gives life to plants, wildlife, and us! Using as little of it as possible not only reduces the energy needed to transport the water from its source, process it, and send it along the pipes to people, but it helps to ensure that there's enough to go around. In this section, we share some water conservation tips that you can apply throughout your home, and then we focus on two places that water tends to flow most freely: the kitchen and the bathroom.

General whole-home tips

Try these general tips to conserve water by reducing the amount you use every day:

- ✔ **Fix leaking faucets right away.** If you can't get to the repair immediately, or if you're waiting for the plumber to arrive, collect the leaking water in a bowl or bucket to use for something else, such as washing the windows or your car or watering your garden or indoor plants.

- ✔ **Install faucet aerators to both kitchen and bathroom taps.**

- ✔ **Check the insulation around water pipes that are exposed to outdoor temperatures to be sure that they won't burst in cold weather.** Don't forget to also check indoor pipes near poorly insulated exterior walls.

In the kitchen

The following tips can help you to avoid wasting water:

- ✔ **When you turn the tap on and wait for hot water, fill a basin or jug with the cold tap water that would normally go down the drain while you wait.** Use this cold water for drinking, cooking, watering your plants, filling your pets' water bowls, pre-rinsing the dirtiest dishes, or rinsing off the dishes after you wash them.

- ✔ **If you prefer your drinking water cold, instead of wasting water by running the tap until the water cools down, keep a bottle or jug of water in the fridge.**

✔ **Avoid using or installing garbage disposals, as they require water in order to operate.** Dispose of food scraps in the trash or compost pile if they're compostable.

✔ **Use as little water as possible when cooking.** Avoid overfilling saucepans when boiling potatoes or pasta, for example.

✔ **Wash the dishes in a bowl or basin placed in the sink rather than in the sink itself.** Filling the sink requires more water than a smaller bowl or basin.

✔ **Use a natural detergent so that you can use the dirty water to water the garden.**

✔ **Wash the cleanest dishes first and work your way up to the dirtiest ones so that you don't have to change the water so often (or at all).**

✔ **Recycle the rinse water by using it to wash windows, floors, or the car, to flush the toilet, or to water the garden.**

In the bathroom

In general, a shower uses about a third of the water it takes to fill your bathtub. However, the amount of water you use for a bath versus a shower really depends on the depth of the water in the tub, whether you have a low-flow showerhead, and how long you stand under the running water. So, whether you prefer showers or baths, keep water conservation in mind and limit the amount of water that you use.

Here are some tips for conserving water while you get sparkling clean:

✔ **Bathe with your partner (sounds like fun!), or schedule baths and showers directly after each other so that hot water doesn't lose its heat sitting in the pipes.**

✔ **Take a shower instead of a bath, but reduce your shower time.** Five minutes is ideal and ten minutes is the max.

✔ **Place a bucket under the tub spout to catch the water flowing while it heats up.** Use the collected water for other tasks such as watering the garden or flushing the toilet.

Toilet flushing accounts for about one-third of all the household water you use, which is especially significant when you consider that you flush drinking-quality tap water down the drain. Environmentally friendly low-flow toilets and dual-flush toilets are now widely available, but whether you have one or not, you can still conserve water in a number of ways:

✔ **Install water-saving devices such as dams or displacement bags in your toilet tank (see Figure 2-1).** These items take up part of the space usually occupied by water, so they reduce the amount of water used with each flush.

✔ **Use recycled water to flush the toilet, such as rainwater collected in the garden or cold water saved from sinks and tubs while you're waiting for the hot water to come through.** Pour the recycled water into the toilet tank (not the bowl) immediately after you flush, as the tank is refilling.

Figure 2-1: Toilet dams and displacement bags conserve water every time you flush.

Green Cleaning

When it comes to cleaning, you can find a greener way to clean just about everything in the home.

Here are the basic rules of green cleaning:

- ✔ **Use as little detergent as possible.**

- ✔ **Save old toothbrushes for scrubbing dirt and stains out of small, difficult-to-reach areas.**

- ✔ **Clean up as you go along so that dirt and grime doesn't get too dried out and encrusted to be removed by natural cleaners.**

- ✔ **Use a carpet sweeper or dustpan and brush instead of your vacuum cleaner for small cleaning operations.**

✔ **Trade aerosol sprays for plastic spray pumps.**
Aerosol sprays no longer contain chlorofluorocarbons, which contribute to damaging the protective ozone layer in the Earth's atmosphere, but they still contain hydrocarbon-based gases.

You can use everyday items you probably already have in your cupboards to clean almost everything in your home — from the stove to the floors, wooden furniture to glass windows, and more.

Although you can try many natural recipes for creating your own cleaning products, you may still want to purchase some greener cleaning and washing products. Many supermarkets and home stores are coming out with their own brands, but some existing brands to look for include Ecover, Method's Free & Clear line, Restore, and Seventh Generation.

 Baking soda is a mild abrasive that's pretty much a wonder cleaner. (You can get large quantities of baking soda at hardware stores.) Use it as you would an abrasive cleaning powder; following are some suggestions:

✔ Brighten up taps and other chrome fittings with water mixed with a little baking soda.

✔ Clean countertops, appliances, and other surfaces with a small amount of baking soda on a damp cloth.

✔ Clean your fridge inside and out with a solution of 3 tablespoons baking soda dissolved in ½ cup warm water. Wipe it all over the fridge with a damp cloth.

- ✔ Clean the inside of your oven by moistening the walls with a damp cloth, sprinkling baking soda on the surfaces, and leaving it for an hour before wiping it off with a cloth.

- ✔ Soak dirty pots and pans in a basin of hot water with 2 or 3 tablespoons of baking soda for about an hour. Then scrub them clean with an abrasive scrubber.

- ✔ For wet red wine or coffee stains, pour soda water on the stain. If that doesn't work, pour baking soda on the stain, rub it in, and then brush it off.

- ✔ Use baking soda on mildew in the shower and on shower curtains. Add just enough water to the baking soda to turn it into a thick paste. Use an old toothbrush for cleaning the grout between tiles.

- ✔ Pour ½ cup baking soda down your kitchen or bathroom drain followed by ½ cup vinegar and then some boiling water. This combination breaks down fatty acids that block drains and helps to keep drains smelling fresh.

 Another common household item that works wonders is vinegar, which clears away grease and deodorizes. Use regular distilled white vinegar (not your expensive balsamic) to:

- ✔ **Clean lime scale off bathtubs, sinks, and shower heads.** Soak the shower head in vinegar and then brush the built-up lime scale off with an old toothbrush.

- ✔ **Wash your windows.** Spray a mixture of equal parts vinegar and water on the windows and wipe them with old, crumpled-up newspaper to shine them up.

- ✔ **Brush around the toilet bowl.** For stubborn marks, sprinkle the toilet bowl with baking soda and follow up by pouring some vinegar on top of it. Be prepared for the bubbling froth that results. Use a toilet brush to scour the bowl clean.

Here are some other items you can use in your general household cleaning:

- ✔ **Borax:** Borax is a natural mineral that's a disinfectant. It's great in the laundry and as a kitchen cleaner. Add it to your laundry powder to whiten and soften discolored towels and other whites. You can buy it in drugstores, supermarkets, and online; for large quantities, head to a hardware store.

- ✔ **Castor oil:** Castor oil is good for conditioning leather. A bit of elbow grease and this natural cleaner brings tired leather to life again.

- ✔ **Cornmeal:** Cornmeal works on grease stains. Just rub in on the stain and then brush it off.

- ✔ **Lemon juice:** Lemon juice works on lime scale on bathroom fixtures. If the stains are stubborn, leave some lemon juice on the mark for a few minutes, or soak a tissue in lemon juice and set it on the problem area. Bottled lemon juice is less trouble than squeezing fresh lemons and works just as well.

- ✔ **Olive oil:** Olive oil takes finger marks off stainless steel, and, when mixed with a little vinegar (about one part vinegar to three parts oil), it makes a good floor polish.

  Use a mixture of lemon, water, and olive oil instead of furniture polish. The proportions you use depends on the wood and how dirty it is; try a spoonful of each to start. Use it as you would any other polish: Wipe it on and then wipe it off with a dry cloth.

- ✔ **Soda water:** Soda water helps remove carpet stains. Simply dribble some on and dab away the stains.

Going Green with Your Toiletries and Cosmetics

Just as all kinds of synthetic chemicals are found in household cleaners, they also can be found in personal-care products and cosmetics. Here are some ways to reduce your consumption of these products and choose greener versions of them:

- ✔ **Reduce the amount of cosmetics and toiletries you use so that you don't have to replace them as frequently.** For example, most people use far more toothpaste than necessary — a blob the size of a small pea is enough. You also can use scissors to cut through tubes such as toothpaste and hand cream when you can no longer squeeze out any contents: There's usually enough still in the tube for another two to three applications.

✔ **Choose items that have little or no packaging and that come in recyclable or refillable containers.**

✔ **Buy products made with organic cotton if possible.** The cotton industry is one of the biggest consumers of agrochemicals in the world, and the cotton is often treated with chlorine.

✔ **Use electric razors or replaceable razor blades so that you don't throw out disposable razors with plastic handles.**

✔ **Look for products that have all-natural ingredients such as plant or vegetable extracts and that don't contain synthetic chemicals.** This isn't easy — there are nearly 10,500 ingredients used in cosmetics and toiletries according to the Campaign for Safe Cosmetics (www.safecosmetics.org), many of which can be toxic under certain circumstances — but it can be done.

✔ **Choose cosmetics that haven't been tested on animals.** Look for manufacturers that have signed onto the Coalition of Consumer Information on Cosmetics, which ensures they will neither conduct their own animal testing nor use ingredients that have been tested on animals. You can find the manufacturers listed at www.leapingbunny.org.

There are plenty of natural products you can use instead of potions made with lots of chemicals. Tea tree oil is a natural antiseptic and disinfectant, for example.

Chapter 3
Minimizing Your Trash and Decluttering Your Life

● ●

In This Chapter

▶ Generating less waste

▶ Giving your possessions a new lease on life

▶ Unloading electronics in an eco-friendly manner

● ●

*F*or many people, trash is "out of sight, out of mind" as soon as it leaves their homes. But that's not the end of trash's journey; it's just the beginning. For every item you throw out, there's hidden waste — the raw materials that went into its production and the resources such as water and energy that fueled the process, from raw materials to finished goods to land-fill. And much of that energy comes from nonrenewable sources.

The green living ideal is to reduce your trash so much that you produce no waste at all. It's far more practical to focus on reducing your trash as much as you can. Zero waste will become more achievable as recycling and packaging practices catch up with today's culture.

In this chapter, we give you tips for reducing your contribution to the trash heap.

Cutting Back Consumption and Aiming for Zero Waste

The best way to reduce waste is to reduce what you buy. Only bring into your home what you really need and know that you'll use — whether it's food, clothes, or electrical appliances. Bringing in less not only reduces the items you eventually have to dispose of, but it also reduces their associated packaging, which is where much of your waste likely originates.

Buy less

Living a simpler lifestyle isn't about doing without or cutting out the things you truly enjoy. It's about knowing the difference between what you "need" and what you "want," but it's also about prioritizing — looking at your days and deciding what's really *important* to you — so you can make better decisions, for both you and your environment, about how you spend your money.

 Keep a journal of everything that you buy for a month or even a week. When you review the journal, you may see patterns of spending that you weren't even aware of. Perhaps you bring home convenience or takeout food more often than you realize, or maybe you make up for a tough day at work by buying yourself a "treat" such as a new piece of clothing for your closet. Simply recognizing these patterns is often enough to help you break out of them.

Another way to scale back your purchases is to opt for good-quality items over mediocre-quality ones. Buying fewer items of good quality keeps your spending in check and doesn't overwhelm your storage space. It also ensures that you're not throwing items out because they've worn out prematurely.

Be mindful of packaging

Keep in mind that the packaging of items you *do* buy is another important part of reducing excess. Choosing products with minimal or recyclable packaging is easy to do without much inconvenience; you can incorporate this awareness seamlessly into your shopping habits with just a little assessment work on the front end.

 Here are some general tips to guide you around the grocery store, where most packaging trash comes from:

✔ **Buy fresh food that doesn't come prepackaged.** Place fruits and vegetables directly into your cart — skip the plastic bags hanging in the produce department.

✔ **Avoid individually packaged items.** For example, buy a larger container of juice and send the kids to school with juice in a thermos instead of those small, individual juice containers. The same goes for prepackaged kids' lunches in plastic trays that have cheese and crackers and such in them; dividing up cheese and crackers at home into reusable containers that can go into lunchboxes reduces waste considerably.

✔ **Opt for items in glass or other recyclable containers instead of plastic containers that can't be recycled.** Basically, try to avoid any plastic that can't be recycled through your local system.

✔ **Avoid aerosol cans altogether if at all possible because you can't reuse or recycle them.** For cleaning and toiletry products, purchase products in pump-action bottles.

✔ **Take your own canvas bags, shopping basket, or reused plastic bags with you when you shop so that you don't load up on more plastic bags.** If you have a choice between paper and plastic bags, choose paper, which is more easily recycled than plastic. Of course, first reuse it if you can, perhaps to wrap parcels for mailing.

Lengthening the Life of Your Possessions

Cutting back on consumption is an important part of waste reduction, and if you're able to hold onto the possessions you already have for longer, you'll reduce even further your need to buy new items and get rid of the old ones. Not only does this practice reduce your waste, but it also saves you money, which is always a good thing!

Reusing and repurposing

You can't reduce your purchases to nothing, but you can look at what you can reuse. Sometimes you can't reuse items in the same way you've been using them because they're too worn out for that purpose; in these situations, find a new purpose for that item, adapting it however you need to.

Most things have more than one use. Here are some ideas to get you thinking creatively about how to reuse or repurpose things that you own:

✔ **Reuse paper that has only been used on one side.** Put the other side through your printer again for rough drafts, use it for your grocery lists, or give it to your children to use as drawing paper.

✔ **Wash plastic food storage bags after use instead of discarding them.** Use hot soapy water to get them clean. Don't reuse bags that have been in contact with raw or cooked meat, though.

✔ **Use empty glass jars as containers in your workshop or as organizers at your desk or elsewhere.** If you drill holes in the lids and screw them to the underside of a shelf, you can attach the jars to the lids to reduce clutter on your work surface.

✔ **Use wrapping paper and gift bags again, and cut down cards to make gift tags.** Fold gift paper and bags carefully so that they store easily and live to wrap again.

✔ **Line recycling boxes, drawers, and cat litter trays with newspapers, magazines, and junk mail instead of plastic liners that you need to purchase.**

✔ **Alter clothes and cultivate your own vintage look by contributing to and shopping at second-hand clothing boutiques.** If you're interested in more ideas for what to do with clothing, check out *Reconstructing Clothes For Dummies,* by Miranda Caroligne Burns (Wiley).

- ✔ **Repair damaged items.** If it's not worth repairing the item — especially with electrical items, where safety is an issue — decide whether it really needs replacing. You can find advice and step-by-step instruction for simple fixes to appliances, electronics, and furnishings, among other things, in *How to Fix Everything For Dummies,* by Gary Hedstrom, Peg Hedstrom, and Judy Ondrla Tremore (Wiley).

- ✔ **Turn small plastic containers into garden pest traps.** Set the plastic container into the ground and fill it with beer to create a baited trap for harmful pests such as slugs.

- ✔ **Cut old, worn clothing into rags for cleaning, dusting, or washing vehicles.**

- ✔ **Turn old pantyhose into plant supports for the garden.** Simply cut off the legs, loop them around plant stems or branches, and then tie them off to stakes.

- ✔ **Use wine corks to create a corkboard.** Check out www.crafterslovecrafts.com/wine-cork-crafts.html for instructions as well as many other ideas for using old corks.

- ✔ **Cut down a king-size sheet that's worn in the middle into a single-size sheet or a few crib sheets.**

Recycling

If all else fails (meaning that you can't reuse or repurpose items), recycle. *Recycling* involves collecting goods that have reached the end of their lives and processing them, their parts, or some of their parts, into the raw materials from which new goods are made.

Because recycling isn't as green as reusing or reducing (which don't emit greenhouse gases), you should try to reduce and reuse first and foremost. Glass can be recycled into bottles, for example, but it has to go through a manufacturing process to get there, and that process uses energy.

Despite the drawbacks, recycling an item is far better than throwing it in the trash. And as states and cities increasingly develop and encourage waste-reduction strategies, recycling will become an even more important part of daily life.

Identifying what you can recycle

Not everything can be recycled (yet), but you should be able to find recycling facilities for these six main categories of household waste:

- **Paper:** Most paper is recyclable, including newspapers, cardboard, phone books, packaging, magazines, catalogs, and wrapping paper.

  Some recycling facilities take paper products such as milk and juice cartons; others don't. Check with your local recycling service provider before you haul your waste for drop-off.

- **Plastics:** Most plastics are recyclable, but recycling rates for plastic tend to be low because of a lack of facilities.

  Check with your local service provider about which plastics it takes for recycling. If the local authority doesn't accept plastics, try to reduce the plastic that you buy and reuse what you already have.

- ✔ **Glass:** Glass items such as car windshields, cooking dishes, and light bulbs aren't usually accepted by local recycling systems. These items may not be recyclable in your area, or you may need to take them to a special drop-off point. Check with your service provider or local government's waste office to find out if there's a special drop-off point near you. For example, compact fluorescent light bulbs aren't usually accepted in local recycling programs, but Home Depot stores collect the used bulbs for their own recycling program, so you can take them to your local Home Depot store.

- ✔ **Metals:** Metal food and drink cans made from aluminum or steel are recyclable. With food cans, wash them out first and remove paper labels — it's worth the extra chore. Aluminum cans in particular are very valuable in terms of recycling material. You can recycle used aluminum foil, too.

- ✔ **Organics:** Some recyclers include organic materials such as yard and kitchen waste in their regular services, whereas others offer seasonal organics recycling, such as Christmas tree drop-off locations after the holiday season.

- ✔ **Textiles:** Many charitable and nonprofit organizations operate drop-off points for textiles like clothes and shoes; you usually find these sites in supermarket parking lots and in the organizations' own business locations. What the groups can't use they generally sell to private firms dealing in textiles.

Paint isn't recyclable, but it's worth a mention in this section because some communities offer a central drop-off point for leftover paints. People can come and pick up the unwanted paint for free, latex paints may be mixed together and reprocessed, and components of oil paints can be reprocessed into fuel (or at least disposed of responsibly if this isn't practical in your location). It's also possible that local organizations such as Habitat for Humanity (www.habitat.org) can use your unwanted paint, so check with your city or town to see if such a service is available.

Finding places to drop off recyclables

Many local governments have well-established recycling programs that either provide curbside pickup at your home or operate neighborhood drop-off points.

If your community doesn't offer government-sponsored services, look for commercial businesses in your area that offer weekly recycling pickup. There's likely to be a fee involved, but it's worth it to divert waste that would otherwise end up in the trash.

Increasingly, stores also are offering recycling services as a response to customer demand. The office-supply store Staples, for example, lets you drop off used batteries, empty printer ink cartridges, and even unwanted electronics such as televisions and computers, and IKEA stores accept batteries for recycling.

To find recycling resources in your community, check with your local government. Earth 911 (http://earth911.org) and the National Recycling Coalition (www.nrc-recycle.org) also can help.

To make it as easy as possible to recycle — and to prevent it from becoming an overwhelming task — set up a home recycling center that works for your family.

Turning Your Garbage into Someone Else's Gold

If you can't reuse something, you don't know anyone who wants it, and you can't recycle it, you may still have alternatives to throwing it out. In terms of being green, offering your used goods to another person reduces waste and fits in with the idea of reusing as much as possible.

Contributing to sweet charity

If you're interested in giving things away to people who have more need for them than you do, you can donate just about anything.

Make sure that anything you give is in good condition, usable, and clean, and that it won't create a problem for the person receiving it.

Following are a few organizations that accept household or clothing items:

- **Habitat for Humanity** (www.habitat.org) accepts tools, building materials, furniture, and appliances in good working order, either for use in homes being built or for resale to the public in order to help raise funds. It also accepts vehicle donations!

- **Lion's Clubs International** (www.lionsclubs. org/EN/index.shtml/vision_eyeglass_ recycling.shtml) conducts eyeglass recycling, collecting used eyeglasses at a number of eyewear chain stores and redistributing them in developing countries.

- **Nike Re-Use a Shoe** (www.letmeplay.com/ reuseashoe) collects worn-out athletic shoes of any brand and processes them into material that's used for sports surfaces such as playgrounds for youth around the world.

- **The Salvation Army** (www.salvationarmyusa. org) operates local centers that accept household and clothing items for resale.

- **Goodwill Industries International** (www. goodwill.org) has local stores that welcome donations of clothing and household items for resale.

- **Hands Across the Water** (www.surplusbooks forcharity.org) collects unwanted books and sends them to schools and libraries that need them around the world.

Trading goods online

Freecycle (www.freecycle.org) was one of the first Web sites to offer members a way of giving unwanted possessions away for free to other members who would make good use of them. This program takes the principles of reducing, reusing, and recycling into cyberspace. Community members who want to find a new home for something, whether it be a chair, a fax machine, or a piano, send an e-mail offering it to local members, who then respond by e-mail. The rule is that everything offered must be free, legal, and appropriate for all ages. Membership in Freecycle is free.

Sharing Is Giving (www.sharingisgiving.org) is a site with a similar purpose, acting as a one-stop source for all free-transfer Web sites.

Disposing of Electronic Goods

As electronic goods such as televisions, computers, cellphones, and computer-driven toys, as well as auto-mobiles, assume a more-prominent position in your home and daily life, they also become more-prominent contributions to your home's waste.

Not only does the fast pace of the technology industry represent huge losses of reuse potential for many elec-tronic items, it also creates a toxic-waste issue because of the components in many of these products. Thankfully, opportunities for reusing and recycling electronic goods are growing significantly.

Find an electronics recycler near you through the National Center for Electronics Recycling at www.electronicsrecycling.org.

Leveling the cellphone mountain

Because cellphones contain toxic materials such as mercury, it's important to keep them out of landfills and incinerators.

Several organizations reprogram retired cellphones so that they can be used free of charge by people, particularly seniors or victims of domestic abuse, to call 911. Other organizations reprogram and sell the phones to raise funds for charity. The following organizations operate such programs:

- ✔ **Collective Good:** www.collectivegood.com
- ✔ **Phones 4 Charity:** www.phones4charity.org
- ✔ **Wirefly:** www.wirefly.org

You also can check with your cellphone provider about a recycling program; many providers collect old phones to reuse parts and to donate to charities.

Getting rid of computers and TVs

You can donate computers for reuse by facilities such as schools and charities, or if your computer is too old to be useful, it can go to a responsible electronics recycler to break down its components for reuse, recycling, and safe disposal.

To find a computer refurbisher or recycling program in your area, check http://earth911.org (in the Find a Recycling Center box at the top of the home page, enter **computer** and then your zip code or city and state) or www.techsoup.org (click Learning Center, then Hardware, and then Ten Tips for Donating a Computer). Some computer manufacturers have established computer recycling programs, and you can also take computers to Staples stores (www.staples.com/sbd/content/about/soul/recycling.html), which participate in an electronics recycling program.

 Whether you donate your computer for reuse or drop it off for recycling, make sure to use hard drive disk-cleaning software to properly erase your files.

The same places that recycle computer monitors in your area likely recycle televisions, too, because their technology is quite similar.

Disposing of an older vehicle

If your old car is no longer in good enough condition to be sold, you may think it's time for the scrap heap, but that comes with some obvious issues. Some of the material that goes into a vehicle can be recycled or reused (the list of potential items includes liquids such as oil and gas, metal, refrigerants from air-conditioning systems, tires, parts, and even windshields), but other material including foams and plastics end up shredded and in landfills.

 Consider donating your older vehicle to charity: You get a receipt for a tax deduction, and the charity sells the car either at auction or perhaps to an auto recycler. Charity Navigator has excellent information about car donation programs at www.charitynavigator.org.

Chapter 4
Making Great Green Diet Decisions

● ●

In This Chapter

▶ Being selective about where your food comes from

▶ Defining organic, genetically modified, and Fairtrade food

▶ Getting important info from food labels

● ●

*E*ating green means knowing where your food comes from, and that involves two issues: how the food was produced, and how it got to you (including what happened to it along the way). To be sure that your food is as green as possible, you need the answers to these questions.

Some scientists advise that if you were to buy locally produced foodstuff — especially from within 12 miles of your home — you would do more for the environment than if you simply bought organic foods from farther afield. Most significantly, you'd save all the greenhouse gas emissions from the transportation of the foods from those distant places. So, if you follow the philosophy of shopping locally and eating organically if possible, you're well on the way to adopting a sustainable diet.

Choosing Your Food Source Wisely

Despite all the arguments about what food is best in terms of health, there's agreement from an environmental point of view that it's best to buy local food. At the heart of all the arguments for eating locally grown produce is the need to cut down on what have become known as *food miles,* the distance food travels from where it's produced to your plate. Transportation (by plane, truck, ship, or train) over what can be thousands of miles results in a lot of carbon emissions. In addition, food that travels a long distance and spends time in storage has fewer nutrients than locally produced food because the sooner you eat something after it's harvested, the more nutrients you get.

In this section, we fill you in on buying locally, and let you know what to do when doing so isn't an option.

Your best bet: Buying locally

Food that flies thousands of miles to the U.S. from other countries is just part of the food miles problem. Even American produce can travel many hundreds of miles before it gets to your plate. Retailers buy from producers and often transport the food over the road to big packaging plants, to huge storage facilities, to distribution centers, and finally to the stores from which you drive it home. To cut down on those miles, you have to buy locally rather than just buy items made in the U.S. The conundrum? The choice of food retailers is almost as great as the choice of food products:

✔ **Locally owned and operated grocery stores:** Big
  businesses have greater buying power than small
  competitors, but they also transport food farther
  to storage and distribution facilities, increasing
  factory and transport emissions and reducing the
  nutritional value of the stored food.

  If your local (and large) grocery store brings in as
  much local and organic produce as possible, then
  by all means, support it. But if it doesn't do that,
  look for other options. The larger stores' buying
  power may translate into lower food costs on the
  shelves, but do what you can — within your
  budget — to purchase more locally and/or organically produced food.

  Head for smaller specialty stores and co-ops,
  many of which sell organic and/or local products.
  You can find co-ops throughout the country
  through www.coopdirectory.org. Check with
  the store to see how local "local" is.

✔ **Local farmers' markets:** Farmers' markets may be
  open one or two days a week during the growing
  season, or they may operate year-round. They
  cater to people who are interested in buying fresh,
  local, and sometimes organic produce.

  At most farmers' markets, you're able to sample
  and buy local fruit and vegetables that are
  in season and talk to the growers about their
  produce — they're usually passionate about the
  subject — so that you know exactly what you're
  buying and eating. At many markets, you also find
  other locally produced food such as meats,

cheeses, and jams and other preserves. You can find details of local farmers' markets at www.ams.usda.gov/farmersmarkets/map.htm or www.localharvest.org.

Note: Not all the produce at a farmers' market is certified organic.

✔ **Local farms:** If you don't have a local farmers' market, you may be able to hook up with a farm not too far away from you that sells its produce straight from the farm or has its own farm store. Even if you live right in the middle of a city, you may find that farmers set up shop temporarily and sell produce straight off their own trucks. (Some farmers even deliver to established regular customers.)

Local Harvest (www.localharvest.org) has lists of family farms and other sources of sustainably grown food.

✔ **Food-delivery services:** Many cities are serviced by companies that deliver fresh fruit and vegetables from local growers, with some specializing in organic produce. Depending on the company, you may be able to sign up for weekly or occasional (on-demand) delivery and order exactly what you want so that you'll know what will arrive on your doorstep.

To find a food-delivery service in your area, do an Internet search for "food-delivery service" and the name of your city. You may want to add *organic* to the search terms.

If you have the time, energy, space, and desire, the greenest option is to grow some of your food yourself using organic methods.

The alternative option: Finding Fairtrade food

The idea of Fairtrade is that more of the money you pay when you buy an item goes to the producers who then can pay their workers better and invest more in their businesses. It's a trading partnership that aims at sustainable development for excluded and disadvantaged producers.

The Fairtrade label ensures that the products it appears on meet the Fairtrade standards. The goods usually cost a little more than equivalent non-Fairtrade goods, but the benefit is knowing that the producers have been treated fairly. The program aims to make sure that:

✔ Producers are paid a fair price that covers their production and living costs so that they have some security, they have long-term contracts and can plan ahead, and their businesses are sustainable.

✔ The extra money you pay goes toward other aspects of the producers' welfare, such as education.

✔ Producers and workers are allowed to join unions and other organizations that can protect their rights and ensure that they have fair working conditions.

✔ No child labor is used.

✔ Production methods are environmentally friendly and pesticide-free.

You can find more information about Fairtrade at www.fairtrade.net.

Explaining Organic

You may think it should be quite easy to explain exactly what is and isn't organic food. But it's not that straightforward. Hundreds of organizations around the world give certificates to say that products are organic, and each has slightly different criteria by which it makes its judgments.

In the U.S., farmers have to meet the USDA definition of organic through the National Organic Program. Basically, the program says that in growing crops and raising animals the organic way, natural substances are allowed and synthetic substances aren't.

Although organic food is produced by greener methods and shouldn't contain pesticides and other substances that could potentially be bad for your health, it's important to note that scientists aren't in agreement about whether organic food is safer and more nutritious than its nonorganic equivalents. In fact, the USDA is careful to point out that the National Organic Program lets consumers know what is and isn't organic; it doesn't make any claims that organic produce is better or safer for you than nonorganic produce. What isn't disputed, however, is that conventional — and especially intensive — farming methods can be much more damaging to the environment than organic methods.

Avoiding chemicals and unnecessary medicines

Organic farming is much friendlier for the Earth and the local economy than mass production of products. Instead of using chemical-based fertilizers to create a high-yield soil, organic farming uses traditional methods of plowing the soil to break down soil compaction that can reduce water and air getting to the plants' roots, rotating the crops to prevent crop-specific diseases or pests from building up in the soil, and growing *cover crops* such as peas or clover that naturally add fertility to the soil in rotation with conventional crops.

Organic farming also emphasizes the use of physical, mechanical, or biological controls to handle weeds, insects, and plant diseases. The lack of chemicals eliminates the risk that dangerous substances will run into nearby rivers, streams, and the water table below, affecting water quality. In turn, you're less likely to be eating any chemicals used to keep bugs at bay and the soil fertile.

When it comes to livestock, organic animals are fed only organic feed along with vitamins and minerals. Growth hormones and antibiotics also are specifically banned in organic food products, although vaccines are allowed.

Letting nature govern production: Say no to genetic modification!

Genetically modified organisms — also known as *genetically engineered organisms* — are living things whose genetic makeup has been changed by the addition of genes from another living thing. This tampering is done primarily to make plants and animals more beneficial to food production, both in terms of quantity and quality. Human intervention in this way, however, carries with it some major concerns that, for the green community, outweigh the pros, including the following:

- ✔ **The unknown:** Genetic engineering is a relatively new concept, so long-term consequences have yet to be determined. And given the amount of time generally needed to link cause and effect in the scientific world, you can safely assume that these consequences won't be identified in your lifetime — and perhaps not even that of your children or grandchildren.

- ✔ **The potential for genetically modified (GM) crops to "contaminate" non-GM crops when their seeds migrate over distances.** Contamination means that GM seeds could begin growing in non-GM areas. The contaminated crops could no longer be considered non-GM, which is a huge issue especially for organic growers who — through no fault of their own — would suddenly be prevented from calling their crops organic.

- ✔ **The potential for organisms, such as insects and viruses, to evolve and become more powerful and overcome the resistant GM animals and plants.**

Plus, GM ingredients might cause toxic poisoning, allergic reactions, antibiotic resistance, and even cancer in humans. Research hasn't proven all the concerns, but there's enough evidence to warrant caution.

GM crops are common in the U.S., and no labeling is required; in fact, it's believed that upwards of 70 percent of foods in U.S. supermarkets contain some element of genetic engineering. It's highly likely that you're eating GM ingredients in your food without even realizing it.

 The best way to find out whether your food choices contain genetically engineered ingredients is to choose local options so that you can talk to the producers and find out from them exactly what went into the food. If you can't do that, then try talking to the managers or owners of local grocery stores — they may not be able to tell you about production methods, but the fact that you asked them may help to convince them that they should pay more attention to this issue.

If you can't buy the groceries you need from your community, try contacting food manufacturers directly. If companies aren't able to categorically deny that they use GM ingredients, chances are good that they use these products.

Some of the foods and ingredients currently subject to genetic modification for reasons such as increasing yield or pest resistance include soybeans, canola, corn, wheat, and milk.

For animals only: Freedom rules!

Organic livestock farming takes into account both the
health of the animals as well as their welfare. Factory
farming concentrates many animals in a limited space,
which can result in an overflow of animal waste on
each farm and the need to use extra water and chemicals to assist in removing the waste. Additional chemical use can lead to chemicals leaching into the soil and
the water table, and it can mean that the animals are
less healthy and may often need to be treated with
antibiotics and other medicines. Organically raised animals, however, must be *free-range,* which means they
have access to the outdoors, including pasture. They
aren't confined within buildings but may be kept in
buildings temporarily for health or safety reasons.

Factory farming methods have evolved to
meet the ever-growing demand for meat.
The organic approach may be slower and less
profitable — animals have room to move and
so fewer animals can be produced from the
same amount of land, for example — but it
produces cleaner and healthier animals.

If you find it difficult to find organic meat, ask
your local butcher to stock some organic and
sustainable options; increased demand
increases supply. The environment will be
better off and your local butcher will have a
guaranteed customer. You also can purchase
food from animals that have been raised in a
sustainable way through the Eat Well Guide at
www.eatwellguide.org. The site has search-
able listings of producers across the country.

Applying Green Ideals When Shopping the Aisles: Reading Labels

Buying food can be confusing, particularly if you're trying to make healthy and sustainable choices. Reading the labels is important because in grocery stores, they're often the only source of information about the content of the food you buy.

Finding food with good nutritional value and ethical production

When buying a food product, find out if it has arrived on the shelf from a sustainable production process by checking out the following information on the label:

✔ **Ingredients list:** Naturally prepared foods are usually low in added salt, sugar, and saturated fats.

✔ **Animals used:** Some animals and fish are protected species due to their near extinction from being over-farmed or culled or from habitat destruction. Go to www.seafoodwatch.org for the best choices for seafood, good alternatives if you can't find the best choices, and species that you should avoid.

✔ **Country of origin:** Somewhere on the label should be a note that says "Product of x." Technically, this tells you the country the food comes from; however, the reality is that this information sometimes can be misleading. It may indicate, for example, where the product was processed and packaged rather than where the original produce actually came from or where it traveled to during the processing. This information isn't apparent on the packaging, so you may have to check sources such as the manufacturer's Web site to find out where it processes its products.

Looking for organic and more on labels

The USDA's National Organic Program has strict rules on what food manufacturers can and can't say regarding organic foods on food labels. Specifically, if a food label has the National Organic Program's seal on it (see Figure 4-1), the producer has been certified under the program.

Figure 4-1: The USDA's seal confirms that a product is organic.

Here are the USDA's labeling terms, with explanations:

- ✔ **100 Percent Organic:** All ingredients in the product are organic.

- ✔ **Organic:** At least 95 percent of the product's ingredients are organic.

✔ **Made with Organic Ingredients:** At least 75 percent of the product's ingredients are organic.

✔ **Organic ingredients noted on the ingredients statement:** Less than 70 percent of the product's ingredients are organic, so the producer can only identify the actual organic ingredients within the ingredients listing on the product label.

Meat packaging has additional terminology that you should be aware of:

✔ **Natural:** The meat may not have any artificial colors, artificial flavors, preservatives, or other artificial ingredients. Natural production doesn't necessarily mean that the animals led the life of Riley outside, gamboling in the fields.

✔ **Grass fed:** It's considered greener (and kinder) if cows are fed primarily on grass or hay rather than on grain, because they can digest grass and hay more easily.

✔ **Free-range:** This means that chickens, for example, weren't confined to cages. There are different degrees of free-range, however — from true free-range where the chickens are allowed to wander in a fairly large space outside to more limited conditions where they may have only short periods outside in an area that's quite small. It may be difficult to tell exactly what *free-range* means when you see it on meat packaging, so if you're looking at a specific product, consider contacting its producer directly for clarification.

54

 The next time you're in the produce aisle, check out the little label that's stuck on the fruit: You should see either a four- or a five-digit code on the label. A four-digit code means that the produce was produced conventionally (it's not organic). A five-digit code that starts with 9 indicates that it's organically grown, and a five-digit code that starts with 8 indicates that it's genetically engineered.

Failsafe ways to buy locally when labels are unclear

If you find no labels on particular foods, or if you find labels with little information, here are a few tips to help you make the greenest food choices:

- **Eat fruit and vegetables in season.** They're more likely to have been grown locally.

- **Avoid exotic foods.** Find out what grows near where you live by checking out local farmers' markets or by visiting the Web site of your state's department of agriculture, and make the most of it. You'll be supporting your local growers.

- **Look for local businesses.** Check out the companies close to you that produce, package, and transport things like bread, rice, milk, and so on.

 Eating green isn't about sacrificing taste or variety or depriving yourself of a taste that you enjoy. If you're making greener choices most of the time, there's more than enough room for an occasional treat from afar.

 With more than 1,400 titles to choose from, we've got a Dummies book for wherever you are in life!

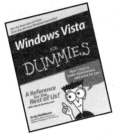